KT-558-166

Dilemmas in Modern Science

T gy

E

th

JON TURNEY

 Contents

Introduction

Humans are pushing the boundaries of science and technology. We can access information at the touch of a button. We can genetically modify food so that it grows faster and tastes better. We have developed medicines that can cure once-fatal illnesses. All this might sound positive, but we are now facing many dilemmas in the areas of science, technology and medicine. Just because we *can* do something, does this mean we *should*?

Many of these debates are based on what is ethically or morally right – for humans, for animals or for the environment. People often feel very strongly about such issues, whether they are governments, pressure groups or individuals. It is important for everyone to understand what these ethical questions are, and to consider the ways in which they might be solved.

The benefits of new technologies can be far-reaching. Improved global communication is just one advantage of satellites orbiting in space.

What is technology?

Many people use the word technology to refer to computers, telephones, MP3 players and other electronic devices. These sometimes get grouped together under the title 'new technology', which suggests that there are a lot of older devices that can be classed as technology, too.

In fact, the first human ancestor who chipped a chunk of flint to make an axe, perhaps two million years ago, started something pretty amazing. People are always coming up with new ideas, so now as well as making fire, weaving cloth or metalworking, there are also space satellites, robots and plasma televisions. The result is a world in which, for people who live in cities at least, almost everything is touched by technology. What that really means is that most things you see around you have been made. 'Technology' covers all the things people make, and how they make them. Through different tools, machines and other devices, humans can control their environments – and sometimes even other people. They can live more comfortable or more interesting lives.

There are concerns that the increasing popularity of computer games means children exercise less than they did before these new technologies became available.

Technological dilemmas

Technology is often talked about in terms of progress, but in the last few decades people have started to ask where developments in technology are taking us. Sometimes real disasters occur, such as when a plane crashes or a chemical plant leaks. More often, technologies that work well have unexpected effects – some good, some bad. Pesticides that protect crops can harm wildlife. Cars, televisions and computer games mean people are now taking less exercise than ever before. Microwave ovens mean that food can be heated or cooked quickly and

families need never sit down together to eat. So, along with all the benefits technology has brought – being warmer and better fed, travelling faster and communicating more easily – there are increasing concerns about the downside of technology.

As modern life is bound up with human inventions, there are often ethical questions that surround the introduction of new technologies. What risks do they come with? Who will benefit? How might they change lives? What choices will they bring? Who should make the decisions?

1 The Age of the Internet

Sometimes technology seems to change very quickly. Just a few years ago personal computers were 'standalone' machines. They could be used for word-processing, running a financial spreadsheet or a database for record-keeping – or just for playing games.

People still use computers for all these purposes, of course, but for most users the important thing is that their computer is connected to millions of other computers all over the world. This is the Internet – a network of networks. It creates endless possibilities. At its most basic, the Internet is an almost limitless source of information. However, more and more people are now using the Internet as a way of communicating, sharing, buying and selling, and presenting themselves in a completely new dimension.

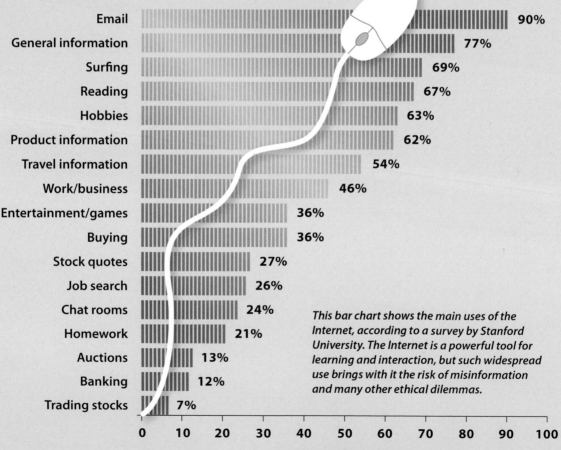

Email	90%
General information	77%
Surfing	69%
Reading	67%
Hobbies	63%
Product information	62%
Travel information	54%
Work/business	46%
Entertainment/games	36%
Buying	36%
Stock quotes	27%
Job search	26%
Chat rooms	24%
Homework	21%
Auctions	13%
Banking	12%
Trading stocks	7%

0   10   20   30   40   50   60   70   80   90   100

Percentage of Internet users

This bar chart shows the main uses of the Internet, according to a survey by Stanford University. The Internet is a powerful tool for learning and interaction, but such widespread use brings with it the risk of misinformation and many other ethical dilemmas.

In most offices today computers are linked (networked) to each other to allow the sharing of files and other information.

Entering cyberspace

The first steps to the Internet came when researchers worked out how to talk to one another on computers connected together locally. Each network had its own codes and controls. In the early 1960s, people began to see the benefits of linking networks in different laboratories or universities. Network links expanded and email grew, first among researchers, then among businesses and private users. However, getting hold of other kinds of information in computer files and finding out where they were stored was difficult for non-experts. The advent of the World Wide Web in 1989 changed all that.

The Internet has become the fastest-growing communications medium in history. Radio took 37 years to reach 50 million listeners in the first half of the twentieth century. Television did it in 15 years. Within three years of the launch of World Wide Web, it had 50 million users.

Who controls the Internet?

The Internet is undeniably a powerful and efficient way of communicating. Like other forms of communication, however, there are many questions associated with it. Who has access to it, and what are they allowed to say? How is the information monitored for accuracy? Who is responsible if someone is offended by the content of a website, or fooled into parting with their money by something they read? The question of responsibility is one of the greatest ethical dilemmas associated with the Internet. Books have authors and publishers – people who take responsibility for the quality and content of their product – but it can be difficult to work out who, if anyone, owns or controls the Internet.

Another major dilemma is how vulnerable to misuse the Internet can be. When exchanging messages online, for example, users can never be sure exactly who they are talking to. Although there are now ways for parents to restrict or monitor their children's use of the Internet, there is still no way of guaranteeing that people are who they say they are in a chat room, or if they will deliver what they promise to on a sales website. It is down to individuals to be aware of the risks and make decisions about their Internet use accordingly.

Wikipedia is an online encyclopedia to which anyone can contribute. Is this a useful way of gaining and sharing knowledge, or an unreliable resource that could result in fiction being presented as fact?

INTERNET USERS
Europe – *322 million*
USA – *233 million*
China – *137 million*
India – *40 million*
UK – *37.6 million*
World – *1.54 billion*

Just one more copy

Ownership of files and information has become a prominent issue as the Internet has expanded in recent years. Although the Internet is intended to make sharing files more efficient, it is important to remember that in most cases someone, somewhere, actually owns the information in those files. Faster transfers, ways of compressing files and clever tricks for piecing together a large file from lots of little bits – which can come from computers in different places – all improve legal uses of the Internet. However, they have also made it very easy to share files that would normally cost money. The music and film industries in particular have suffered from copyright theft through Internet use.

In 2005, major film companies and recording studios in the United States won a Supreme Court ruling that free online music file-sharing services could be sued if their users pirated songs or films. This persuaded several firms to shut down. The US record industry association, the RIAA, has sued over 18,000 people for sharing songs online, and often makes people pay for the files found on their computers.

Napster was founded by Shawn Fanning (pictured at a press conference) as a music file-sharing site. Users could copy mp3 files from other people's computers. In 2001, a Court of Appeal ruled that Napster had to prevent its subscribers sharing material that was in copyright.

Most music can now be downloaded and paid for over the Internet, and this is often cheaper than buying it from a shop. Sales of CDs have declined dramatically, and one day in the near future they will seem as old-fashioned as vinyl records or cassette tapes.

Controlling Internet piracy

Sales of compact discs are falling – a trend that began in 1999 when the free online file-sharing service Napster began working. Today, though, this is more to do with the success of online music sales than piracy. Music companies are optimistic that their lawsuits have managed to bring Internet-assisted copying under control. At the moment, legal copyright on music runs out after 50 years in Europe, so it is permitted to download free copies of older recordings. However, record companies and some musicians are pressing for copyright protection to be extended beyond 50 years. They argue that people who made records 50 years ago are often still alive, and deserve to go on benefiting from their work.

Printed books seem to have largely escaped the threat of Internet piracy. This is probably because people who want to read a whole book will still print it out, so they might as well buy a paperback. If technologists come up with 'electronic books' that are as easy to read as the traditional kind, this may well change and a new dilemma over information ownership will arise.

YOU DECIDE

These days it is very easy to find songs on free file-sharing networks and to download them without paying a penny.

? *Most popular bands make their living from selling records. Is it fair to take away their income by downloading music for free?*

? *If you pay to see a band live, for example, you are supporting them anyway. Does this make it acceptable to take advantage of these free downloads?*

? *If everyone else is doing it, and the files are available anyway, should you just see it as the modern way of expanding your music collection?*

A digital divide?

The ethical issues surrounding the Internet are not limited to content control and ownership. There is also the possibility that as the Internet spreads, its use may reinforce existing inequalities. Printed books are no use if you cannot read. In the same way, the Internet is only a valuable tool if you have a computer with high-speed access. Not everyone does.

There are differences within countries, but these are difficult to assess accurately. Many people in developed countries now have a fast broadband connection at home, accessible through a home wireless network that is always on. However, others in the same country might have older computers and slow or unreliable connections. They may not have a home computer at all, and will have to go to an Internet café and pay by the minute. In the United States, for example, in 2003 54 per cent of white students used the Internet at home, compared with 26 per cent of Hispanic and 27 per cent of African-American youngsters.

International inequalities

There are also big differences between countries. At the end of 2006, there were more than one billion Internet users worldwide – or roughly one in six people. Half of them were in Europe (322 million users) and the United States (233 million). But the percentage of the population in individual countries with Internet

access ranged from a low of 0.1 per cent in the Congo to a high of 77 per cent in New Zealand.

This uneven distribution is likely to worsen existing inequalities in access to information and differences in wealth between nations. Better communication networks are vital for improving healthcare and education in less developed countries. These are the places where they are most needed, but least available.

Steps are being taken to address this dilemma. One effort is backed by the Bill and Melinda Gates Foundation, founded by Microsoft billionaire Bill Gates. In 2006, the Foundation pledged $328 million to provide computer and Internet access through public libraries in developing countries.

Controlling the net

While some countries are trying to improve access to the Internet, others are more interested in restricting it. Their governments want to stop citizens using it for things they disapprove of. The country that most combines rapid growth in Internet use with the strongest controls is China.

Although China has more than 137 million Internet users, the government restricts the information available to them. It prevents access to certain websites, and censors the personal web diaries called blogs, bulletin boards and email messages.

There are strict laws there about what people can do and say online, and technical controls to back them up. The Chinese authorities employ thousands of people to monitor websites, and they make Internet service providers do the same. Asking a Chinese-based search engine for information about the Tibetan religious leader the Dalai Lama, for example, will not lead to any websites written outside the country. Is it morally right for a government to restrict information in this way, or should it be equally available to everyone around the world?

GOOGLE

The leading Internet search company Google announced in 2005 that it was establishing a Chinese-based service, which blocks access to websites blacklisted by the Chinese government. The company says this is the best way of improving access to information on most subjects for Chinese users. Users of the special China service will be informed when a search has returned restricted results, but will not be able to see which sites have been left off the list.

In 2006, Google agreed that it would block search terms that were considered sensitive by the Chinese government.

" *Google's objective is to make the world's information accessible to everyone, everywhere, all the time.* "

Elliot Schrage
Vice-president, Global Communications and Public Affairs, Google Inc.

Technology at work and school

The new technologies and communications systems in place today undoubtedly increase efficiency in schools and workplaces, and have allowed instant global interactions between companies and individuals, as well as providing a valuable educational resource for children. In the early days of email, no one could have predicted the scale on which it would revolutionise business, or indeed personal relationships. But technology in the workplace has brought with it a number of ethical dilemmas for the people who create, manage and use it.

Questions of privacy

In many offices where computers are networked, it is often possible to access files and information belonging to someone else. This is simple and time-efficient. However, it also means that people may be able to see private files that are not intended for public view or use. Employers may be able to access any file on any computer and find out personal information about their employees, even to the point of seeing what web pages they have recently looked at. If the computers are owned by the employers, are they within their rights to view any information stored on them? Or do employees have the right to some level of privacy, even at work?

In some companies, emails are monitored automatically and are scanned for particular words that might indicate that email contains something inappropriate. If it turns out that the email has been sent from a friend, the intended recipient can be held responsible and may face disciplinary action from his or her employers. So, where do we draw the line between acceptable monitoring to ensure a good working practice, and an invasion of the privacy that we have come to expect as a basic human right?

Children now have access to the Internet at school and often at home, too. This can be a valuable research tool, but also offers opportunities to cheat at homework by plagiarising other people's work.

WORKPLACE PRIVACY
Workers in the European Union are protected by a law that says companies cannot monitor their employees' use of email or the Internet unless they have made it clear that they have a policy of doing so, or without gaining employees' consent. For example, in 2007 the European Court of Human Rights ruled in favour of an employee at a Welsh college, who sued her employers for breach of privacy rights after they secretly monitored her emails. In the United States there is no such law in place, and employees are not protected against companies disciplining them for what is regarded as misuse of this technology.

The Love Bug computer virus began in Asia and then swept through America and Europe. It was sent in the form of an email called 'I Love You', with an attachment. Once the attachment was opened, the virus took hold and forwarded the email to everyone in that person's email address book.

YOU DECIDE

Ethical questions are not just found in the workplace. Schools must also be aware of the moral dilemmas that modern technology can pose. For example, access to information means students can 'cheat' when doing coursework. They can simply copy and paste information and pretend it is their own work.

? *Is this just the modern way of researching or is it plagiarism?*

? *Where is the line between using the Internet to get information, and stealing other people's ideas?*

? *Is copying from the Internet justified as long as you are learning new things?*

Virus spreading

Another major issue arising from a greater reliance on technology in the workplace is the spreading of viruses – programs designed to invade and infect computers, causing information to be irretrievably lost. These viruses are most commonly spread via email, and can be catastrophic for companies and individuals if information has not been backed up. The people who create viruses do so for no other reason than to cause havoc. This new type of crime has raised an important question – do we rely too heavily on modern technology? It can be argued that, in the western world, we live in a culture where communications are predominantly electronic and we feel helpless when that technology lets us down. Is it time to reassess the risks and move into a future where the uses of email and the Internet are more carefully controlled and perhaps limited? Or should we be encouraging the development of even more advanced technologies that would reduce the vulnerability of email and Internet use?

2 Who Has Your Information?

With so many computers now connected across the globe, it is easier than ever to find out personal information about other people. Everyone deals with doctors' surgeries, banks or shops. All these places keep records, usually on computers. One of the biggest ethical and practical dilemmas to arise from today's technology is how access to personal information can and should be controlled.

We live in a world where many of our actions are recorded and can be monitored – whether we are aware of it or not. Closed-circuit TV cameras spot you as you enter or leave a shopping mall. Mobile-phone companies record what calls you have made and where you were when you made them.

If you use a 'loyalty card' in a supermarket, the store will use it to build up a profile of your shopping habits. Sometimes people can be surprised when old information finds new uses. Supermarket loyalty cards let stores reward regular shoppers, and make special offers to the right people. Usually, they give points worth a few pennies for every pound spent – although some stores in the United States actually charge more to customers without the right card.

The information that accumulates when things you buy are put through the checkout is very detailed. One customer who found this out was an American shopper whose recorded purchases of expensive wine were used as evidence in court to show that he could afford to pay more money to his ex-wife! Supermarkets and other stores are also now experimenting with tiny radio-frequency identity tags, which will mark their goods. This is a stock-control and anti-theft device, but it could also mean someone going through your wardrobe could tell where every single item you have came from, and when it was bought.

The 'Pay by Touch' scheme is the latest method of paying for your shopping. It is a biometric system that uses a fingerprint scanner, which is linked to a database that holds information about the individual's bank account and loyalty-card details. This means it is impossible for someone to pay for shopping using a stolen card.

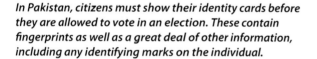

In Pakistan, citizens must show their identity cards before they are allowed to vote in an election. These contain fingerprints as well as a great deal of other information, including any identifying marks on the individual.

Identity theft

One of the most worrying consequences of this availability of information is identity theft. This is when people use computers or other means to find out personal information, such as bank details, and then use them as though they were their own. Once an identity thief has got hold of a credit-card number, for example, it is very easy for them to buy things online using that card, as no pin number or signature is required.

So much information is stored on computers these days that clever hackers can often find ways of accessing it and using it to their advantage. Many companies, especially banks, are constantly improving security on their websites so that people can do their online banking without fear of other people discovering their passwords or other access information, but they find it is a constant race to keep ahead of the thieves.

YOU DECIDE

In some countries a universal ID card has been introduced. These are linked to a biometric record – a fingerprint or an iris print – and produced whenever someone uses health, welfare or other services.

? *Should records like this be linked with other government databases, containing information about health, social-security payments, employment, or criminal records? If so, which ones?*

? *Whose responsibility should it be to check that the information is accurate?*

? *Who else might have access to this information and who should control this access?*

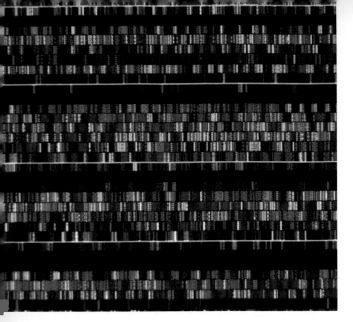

The sequence of a person's DNA can be shown as a sort of 'barcode'. The pattern is different for each individual except identical twins.

> **There is the long-term risk that people can get into these samples and start teasing out additional information about a person's paternity or risk of disease. The police have absolutely no right to that sort of information.**
>
> Alec Jeffreys
> *Developer of DNA fingerprinting*

The fight against crime

Although this collecting and storing of personal information can be seen as an invasion of privacy and a violation of human rights, there are many advantages to technology that allows such information to be stored and recalled when needed. The fight against crime and terrorism is one area in which information storage and retrieval can be useful. Rises in crime rates in many countries mean that people are under closer watch than ever before. There may be people listening in on phone conversations, reading emails, checking which websites have been accessed or investigating bank records. And there are fast-growing databases of DNA samples for personal identification, which help the police in criminal investigations.

DNA fingerprinting

The basic principles of DNA fingerprinting were worked out by the British scientist Alec Jeffreys in 1985. Starting with a biological sample such as blood, semen, hair or skin, the genetic material – the DNA – is extracted and mixed with special enzymes. These recognise particular sequences of the chemical building blocks in DNA. Everyone's DNA is slightly different and the fragments produced have different lengths. They can be separated and compared with the pattern of fragments from a known sample. A match gives a very good chance that the two samples come from the same person. If the first sample came from a crime scene, a match is powerful evidence that the person identified was there. Computer matching can now check crime samples against millions of DNA records in a database. All this sounds like a positive step in solving crimes. However, DNA testing is not 100 per cent accurate and can therefore only be used to *suggest* someone's involvement in a crime – it cannot prove it beyond doubt. Some people think that DNA testing should not be permitted because of this margin of error. There is another factor involved in the DNA testing dilemma – the development of this technology has brought to light many wrongful convictions. People who have spent years in prison are now being released on the basis of new DNA evidence.

A 'Big Brother' society

There are therefore many ethical questions about the use of DNA technology. It can certainly help to solve crimes and to confirm the innocence of wrongly convicted people, but it is not infallible. Should courts be allowed to accept evidence based on DNA testing? Should everyone have to give a DNA sample to create a worldwide database that would allow police to instantly identify a suspect? There are fears that governments and organisations like the police having access to personal information like this will gradually result in a 'Big Brother' system like the one in George Orwell's novel *1984*, which could be used to control people and make them conform.

Forensic science has been helped immensely by DNA fingerprinting. DNA can be extracted from blood or hair found at a crime scene, and then compared with samples taken from suspects or those already on a database.

YOU DECIDE

People arrested on suspicion of committing a crime in some countries may have to give a DNA sample to the police. This will be kept on a database even if the person is not charged with the crime. In Germany and some other countries, 'innocent' samples are destroyed when the investigation is over.

? *Is it right to keep samples in the belief that a larger database will solve more crimes?*

? *Are people whose samples are kept now 'guilty until proven innocent'?*

? *Would it be fairer if everyone was on the database, so the sample collection was unbiased, or is this a needless expense and a violation of human rights?*

Surveillance cameras can be seen everywhere today. Security services are experimenting with facial-recognition systems that may be able to identify individuals, and high-resolution cameras that can zoom in on details like print in a newspaper.

The eye on a pole

One of the most obvious signs that we are being watched is the presence of closed-circuit (CCTV) cameras – in shops, car parks and in the streets. These can be used to monitor crowds and traffic, or to tell a train driver it is safe to close the doors. They can show a security guard who is at the door of a building or they can inform the police when a fight has broken out outside a bar.

Cameras and computers together can do more. The financial district of London, the 'City', was shaken by an IRA bomb blast in 1993. It is now surrounded by cameras linked to a number-plate recognition system, which can check 100,000 vehicles a day against a national database. The same technology is now used to back up London's Congestion Charge, which people pay to drive their cars into the city centre. Around two million new cameras are bought each year in the United States, most by private buyers. But there is increasing use of cameras in public areas in the USA, too.

Active monitoring and recording of camera feeds is also spreading. People who the watchers think look suspicious can be followed throughout their visit to a shopping mall, for example. It is also becoming more common for extracts from security recordings to find their way into television programmes or on to the Internet, where they can be viewed by millions.

> **❝ Mass surveillance is not the answer to the problem of terrorism, and not a road that any nation should be heading down. What is needed is good intelligence on specific threats – not the so-called 'risk-profiling' of entire populations. ❞**
>
> *Tony Bunyon*
> *Director of the US civil liberties group Statewatch*

Civil liberties

People who support such systems say they enhance security, help prevent crime and improve detection. Those with nothing to hide have nothing to fear. The price is a loss of privacy, and the knowledge that you may be caught on camera when you are doing something that is legal, but you would not necessarily want others to know about.

All these issues raise ethical questions about personal privacy and who has the right to know. The rise in terrorism in recent years has resulted in governments all over the world using such monitoring systems to record a great deal of information. Civil liberties groups such as ICAMS (International Campaign Against Mass Surveillance) are calling on governments and other international organisations to limit what they see as an infringement of the human right to privacy. Governments argue that national security should take priority over personal feelings. Should individuals put aside any discomfort they might feel about being 'watched' if the growth in mass surveillance might solve a crime or prevent a terrorist attack?

RFID TAGGING

Some schools in Japan use RFID (radio frequency identification) tags for pupils, so their parents know when they arrive in school or leave for home. One Californian school has already introduced a system where pupils wear RFID badges all the time, to simplify attendance-taking and to help reduce vandalism. In early 2006, a security company in Ohio, USA, implanted two of its workers with RFID chips under their skin so that they would have automatic access to buildings.

In countries such as Germany, RFID tags are being used as security devices in shops. These tags will eventually replace barcodes.

3 Technology and the Military

The earliest tools made by humans – such as flint axes – were probably used for butchering animals, but they could easily double as weapons. Many modern technologies, like aeroplanes, have had both peaceful and warlike uses. Other technologies, however, have been specially developed to make it easier to kill people. Military uses of technology have been the source of great moral and ethical debate.

Smart bombs, defoliants (super weed-killers used to strip jungle cover in Vietnam), penetrating munitions, napalm for firebombing, phosphorus, mines – these weapons are examples of warfare already being used in countries around the world. But where is this technology taking us? What comes next? Should we go on developing such weapons for our own national defence or for selling to other countries? Most importantly, where does the power lie in making decisions on these difficult issues?

This photograph was taken in 1970 during the Vietnam War and shows an area of trees devastated by napalm. Although using napalm was an effective method of revealing enemy positions, thousands of civilians were killed in the attacks.

Bombs and bomblets

Some older-style weapons are still in use and continue to present ethical problems over and above those involved in any war. One controversial example is cluster bombs, in which one bomb releases lots of smaller ones. The tiny bomblets are designed to spread over a wide area. Cluster bombs were first used by the Germans in the Second World War, but since then they have become a standard weapon used by the military in many countries. More modern versions appeared in the 1960s, and hundreds of millions were dropped in Laos, Cambodia and Vietnam during the Vietnam War. The British Army used them in the Gulf War in 1991. Today, such bombs are still being used by American forces in Iraq.

Advantages and disadvantages of cluster bombs

Different types of cluster bombs contain different kinds of bomblets. Some of these are designed to kill or maim people by exploding into lots of fragments. Others are anti-tank weapons, designed to blow up armoured vehicles.

Groups such as Oxfam and Amnesty International claim that not all the bombs work, and many unexploded devices are left lying around – often far from the intended target. Some bomblets are brightly coloured, and children may play with them. The nature of cluster bombs means that they can affect quite a large area, rather than targeting specific buildings. This can result in large numbers of civilian casualties. Governments argue that they are an effective method of warfare, destroying targets over a wide area. Increasing public pressure has led to many countries reconsidering their position on the use of cluster bombs.

An unexploded cluster bomblet in Laos, Southeast Asia. Unexploded bombs are a huge hazard in some places, as they could go off at any time, killing or injuring people nearby.

 Cluster bombs not only kill and maim civilians caught in the crossfire, but like landmines, they leave a deadly legacy, destroying lives and livelihoods for years afterwards. It is time the world banned one of the most indiscriminate weapons of war. **"**

Anna Macdonald
Conflict campaign manager, Oxfam

> ### BAN THE BOMB
> *Belgium is the only country at the moment that has a complete ban on the production, trade and transport of cluster bombs. However, in February 2007, during talks in Oslo, Norway, 46 nations – including the United Kingdom – agreed to discuss terms of a treaty that would commit them to banning these weapons. Of the countries present, only Japan, Poland and Romania refused to commit to the declaration.*

Remote warfare – rich and poor

Much current development in military technology uses new computer and information technology to wage war remotely – that is, from a distance rather than at close range. There are automated planes, 'drones', for keeping watch, and robot vehicles. Cruise missiles can be guided to targets hundreds or thousands of kilometres from launch.

    The idea of developing such weapons is to protect pilots and ground troops, and save lives. Certainly remote warfare has helped in this way. But could this 'low-risk' method of fighting actually encourage more use of weapons against enemies who lack such technology? For example, in 2003, near the start of the war in Iraq, the Iraqis did not have cruise missiles or the resources to develop them. They had no way of countering cruise-missile attacks from their enemies, which put them at a disadvantage. There can be a great discrepancy in the technological weaponry available to developed and developing countries.

This chart shows the amount of money spent on military technology in the key areas of the world, as a percentage of total government spending. North America alone spends almost half of this. This reflects the divide between wealthy and poorer nations, who do not have the resources to develop advanced military technology.

MILITARY EXPENDITURE

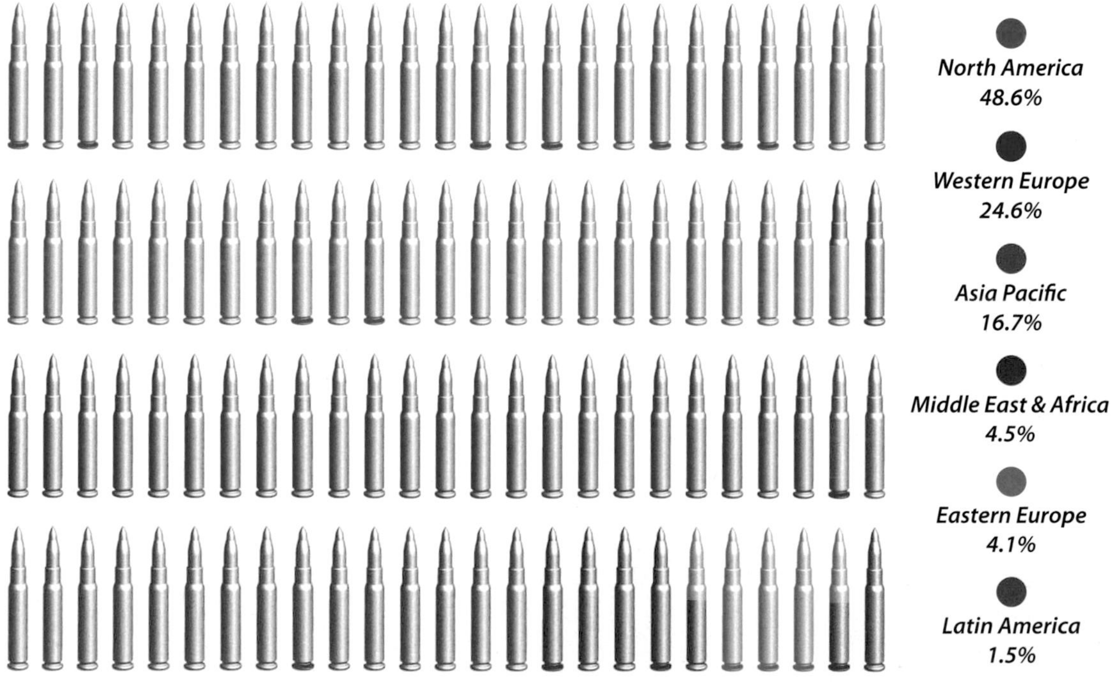

North America
48.6%

Western Europe
24.6%

Asia Pacific
16.7%

Middle East & Africa
4.5%

Eastern Europe
4.1%

Latin America
1.5%

Cruise missiles are a deadly form of remote weapon. Many developed countries use them in warfare but increasingly, developing countries are building them. This is a test on a cruise missile in Pakistan.

Human distance and human error

Another issue surrounding remote warfare is that killing an enemy remotely almost seems like a computer game – it is quite different from looking someone in the eye and pulling the trigger. Some groups argue that this results in a lack of moral conscience about military action because the people conducting the attacks are so distanced from the effects – they do not directly witness the consequences of their actions.

There is also a real danger that the wrong target could be hit when using automatic programmed weapons – even remote weapons are only as accurate as the information they are given, and as a result they are subject to human error. In 1999, during the war in Kosovo, NATO bombed the Chinese embassy by mistake, killing three people and injuring many more. Some estimates suggest that as many as 20 per cent of remote weapons do not reach the targets for which they are intended.

ROBOTIC SECURITY

The technology company Samsung, with Korea University, has developed a robot sentry, armed with a machine gun. The machine has two cameras – one for daytime and one for night – and can zoom in on objects of interest. A computer brain distinguishes

between people and other objects like trees, and a loudspeaker warns any intruder to surrender or be shot. The South Korean government may use the robots on the border between North and South Korea. This could be bad news for any passers-by who are refugees rather than soldiers from the North, and may not understand what the robot is for.

The ultimate defence

Ethical questions can also arise when technology is used purely for defence. Nuclear weapons were invented and used in the Second World War. They have never been used since then, even though there are now thousands of nuclear warheads. Many believe this is because using a nuclear weapon would provoke a nuclear strike on the attacker – with horrific consequences. This idea is known as 'deterrence'. During the years of the Cold War between the former Soviet Union and the United States – when both built huge stockpiles of nuclear bombs and rockets – deterrence was renamed Mutually Assured Destruction (MAD). It seemed to be effective.

In that stable state, could developing an effective defence against nuclear weapons be dangerous? Originally, both the United States and the Soviet Union agreed that it might be, and the two countries signed an anti-ballistic missile (ABM) treaty in 1972, limiting the development of such systems.

Although nuclear weapons have been the source of controversy since their development during the Second World War, many countries still see them as an effective defence mechanism. This nuclear warhead is being paraded through the streets of New Delhi in India.

Star Wars

In the 1980s, however, US President Ronald Reagan launched a research programme to find ways of shooting down missiles. This was called the Strategic Defence Initiative – but it was nicknamed 'Star Wars' after the film. Although the prototype missile interceptors did not really work, the research continues today, under a later programme authorised by presidents Bill Clinton and George Bush. This is now aimed at defending the United States against missile attacks from countries that have – or might get hold of – a small number of nuclear warheads, such as North Korea or Iran.

Supporters of the later programme point out that, unlike Star Wars, it does not mean putting weapons into space – the attacking missiles may be tracked from space but would be shot down by smaller, faster rockets launched from the ground, or possibly by ground-based lasers (intense light beams). There is still controversy about whether the system will ever be fast, accurate and reliable enough to work.

The next generation?

In 2002, the US government awarded $50 million to the Massachusetts Institute of Technology (MIT) for the Institute for Soldier Nanotechnologies. The Institute is working on a range of projects to help develop a 'twenty-first century battle suit'. The aim is a soldier who has effective, lightweight armour, and is protected against chemical and biological weapons. The suit would also be able to sense wounds and provide basic medical care until the soldier could be taken to a field medical station. Although this may prevent loss of life in a battle situation, should we be focusing on resolving differences between nations rather than developing ways of more efficient and deadly fighting? Or is it idealistic to believe such conflict can be resolved?

Greenpeace activists in Japan demonstrate against the 'Star Wars' programme initiated by the United States.

66 ***It is the policy of the United States to deploy as soon as is technologically possible an effective National Missile Defense system capable of defending the territory of the United States against limited ballistic missile attack (whether accidental, unauthorized, or deliberate).*** 99

US National Missile Defense Act, 1999

YOU DECIDE

It can be difficult to decide whether military technology should be developed even further as a deterrent against future attacks or as a defence if they should occur.

? *Is it acceptable to invest money in military technology as long as the weapons systems are intended for defence rather than attack?*

? *Should remote weapons be banned on ethical grounds because their accuracy cannot be guaranteed, or are civilian casualties a necessary part of warfare?*

? *Is military technology acceptable because it enhances national security?*

Recently there have been calls for stricter regulations about how nanotechnologies are developed and applied, to ensure that risks are accurately assessed and the benefits are made available to all.

How is nanotechnology controlled?

One of the biggest concerns about nanotechnology is that there is no central governing body that controls how this latest science is developing. Governments in many countries have commissioned independent bodies to investigate the implications on human health and the environment – including the Food and Drug Administration and the Environment Protection Agency in the United States, the Royal Society/Royal Academy of Engineering in the United Kingdom, and the Federal Institute of Risk Assessment in Germany.

Organisations such as the Nanoethics Group and the International Council on Nanotechnology are investigating the ethical implications of all the latest developments in nanotechnology. They try to take an objective view, accepting that there are both benefits and drawbacks to this type of technology, and weighing them up against each other. They hope to educate more people about the ethical issues, which is a step in the right direction – but they cannot control the policies of individual countries.

NANOTUBES

One of the most promising areas of nano-technology is the development of nanotubes. These are made of carbon atoms, linked together in a repeating pattern of five and six-sided shapes, with a hollow centre. They are very light and much stronger than steel. They also conduct heat and electricity very well. Some car manufacturers use paint blended with nanotubes, which can be electrified so that it sticks to the metal of a car body. Nanotubes are also likely to find their way into faster, smaller computers.

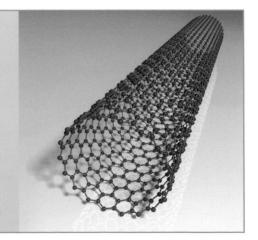

Who will benefit from nanotechnologies?

Like any new technology, any costs and benefits of nanotechnologies are likely to be spread unevenly. Cheap, efficient ways of purifying water or converting solar energy could be great for developing countries, for example. Although, because of its costs, most nanotech development is likely to happen in countries that already have 'high-tech' industries, several developing nations – including Costa Rica, Bangladesh, Brazil, China and India – are investing in the research and development of nanotechnologies. This is not all good news, though: nanotech computers and other devices might transform products in these countries and lead to economic upheaval. As with information technology and the Internet, some see the possibility of a divide between countries with lots of experts in nanotechnology, and those without.

There has been a huge increase in spending on nanotechnologies over the past 10 years or so. The United States and Japan are leading the way, but most developed countries and some in the developing world are spending more on this new technology.

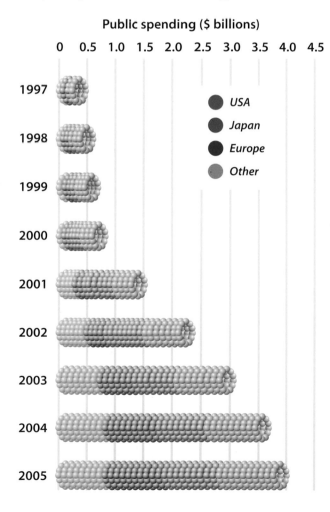

Public spending ($ billions)

Legend: USA, Japan, Europe, Other

Years: 1997, 1998, 1999, 2000, 2001, 2002, 2003, 2004, 2005

Axis: 0 0.5 1.0 1.5 2.0 2.5 3.0 3.5 4.0 4.5

YOU DECIDE

The possibilities of nanotechnology might be beneficial in many ways, and it seems unlikely that its progress can be stopped, but there are several questions that must be addressed before developments get too far.

? *Do nanotechnologies need new regulations that require proof of safety before they can be marketed, or should we consider that although the hazards are unknown they might not be real?*

? *How can the potential dangers of nanotechnology, such as its use for making weapons, be minimised?*

? *Is it the responsibility of nations who have developed beneficial nanotechnologies to share them with other countries?*

5 Robots and Automation

One of the most obvious benefits of technology is the way in which it makes jobs easier and more efficient for humans. As technology developed and designers thought up new ways of controlling machines, devices were created that could work alone with just a few basic instructions. A simple example of this is that instead of a bowl of water and suds, and a hand wringer for drying, we now use a washing machine that runs through a pre-set cycle at the touch of a button. It does what it does automatically. When a whole factory works the same way, it is called automation.

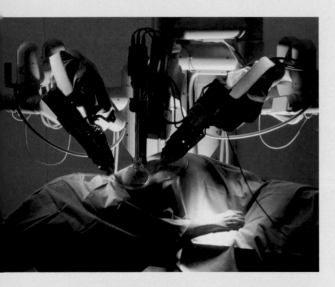

Today, robots can perform extremely advanced tasks. The Da Vinci robot can perform surgery, manipulated remotely by doctors. This could be used, for example, if an astronaut suffered an injury while in space.

The rise of the machine

Some automated machines now perform tasks completely on their own – these are robots. The word comes from the Czech writer Carel Kapek's play *RUR* (Rossum's Universal Robots), written in the 1920s. His robots, like most of those in science fiction, looked a bit like humans. However, there is no reason for real robots to have two arms, two legs and eyes in front. They might also be better than people at some tasks – they can be stronger, faster or more accurate. Technology has advanced so much in recent years that some scientists and engineers predict robots may one day be more intelligent than people. At the moment, the ethical dilemmas arising from the development of robots and automation are largely based on efficiency and employment. But if more advanced computers and computer-controlled robots are created – with 'artificial intelligence' (see page 36) – many new dilemmas may arise.

> 66 *The first rule of any technology used in a business is that automation applied to an efficient operation will magnify the efficiency. The second is that automation applied to an inefficient operation will magnify the inefficiency.* 99

Bill Gates
Founder of Microsoft

Machines at work

One of the earliest-known dilemmas about machines and work occurred 200 years ago, early in the Industrial Revolution. Some spInners and weavers formed a group to destroy new machines that they believed were causing fewer jobs, lower wages and less skilled work for humans. The movement took the nickname of an early leader, Ned Ludd, and people opposed to new technology are often called 'Luddites' today.

At work, it is true that machines have improved productivity and prosperity. Even poorer people in wealthy countries have more material belongings than anyone dreamed of owning in 1800. Beyond that, though, it is difficult to say just what the effects of automation on jobs have been. When unemployment is high, some people fear that mechanisation will drive more people out of work, but others argue that making factories or offices more productive will increase prosperity. In developing countries, it is possible that machines imported and used by large multinational companies are driving local people out of essential jobs, but the same argument about long-term advantages could still apply.

Luddites destroy weaving machinery in a textile factory during the Industrial Revolution. They feared they would be put out of work by this modern technology.

A telerobot is an electronic puppet, controlled remotely by a human using a computer and devices such as joysticks and high-tech gloves. These could have many applications – this one is being developed to work deep under the ocean.

YOU DECIDE

Since automated machines were first developed there has been a division between people who believe they are positive, labour-saving devices and those who believe they are negatively affecting the role of people in the workplace.

? *Is unemployment a valid argument against the development of new technologies?*

? *Where might the line be drawn between technologies that have a wider social benefit and those that simply allow us to be 'lazy'?*

? *If it might one day be possible to 'telecommute', should local labour laws such as minimum wage apply to overseas workers?*

Robots learn new tricks

One of the most significant changes in factory mechanisation came in the first half of the twentieth century. The assembly line was pioneered by Henry Ford to make millions of his famous Model T Ford. There was no longer the need for skilled mechanics to collect the parts and build a car in a workshop. On an assembly line, partly built cars rolled down a track and workers each did one or two of the hundreds of jobs required to finish them off, in the same order for each car. This was the basis of cheap mass production, but the jobs on the line were often dull, repetitive and stressful.

Later, industry pioneers realised that car production was well-suited to the first industrial robots. Spray-painting body parts, welding the chassis and tightening wheel nuts are all tasks that can be turned into a set series of movements for a machine.

MIPS

Whether or not computers can outperform the human brain depends on two factors: how fast the machine can work and the software that powers it. One standard way of measuring computer power is in millions of instructions per second – MIPS. The latest chips used in personal computers can manage approximately 10,000 MIPS. Lots of processing chips can be placed in one computer, but organising them can be complex. Some real breakthroughs in computing technology will be needed before computers will truly be more advanced than the human brain.

Car production lines are still the places where most robots work. There are roughly one million industrial robots now installed in factories around the world.

Robots vs. humans

It might seem like a simple equation – more robots means less work for humans – but the dilemma is more complicated than this. So far, development of machines has not led to incurable unemployment. For example, around five million jobs have been lost in manufacturing in the United States since 1979, but these losses cannot only be blamed on the rise of technology – they were also due to dips in the economy and companies shifting production to cheaper countries. Is technology just one factor among many that have caused a change in the modern workplace?

It is not only unemployment that has caused concern among detractors of robotic development, though. They also point to the fact that work changes as new technologies are developed, and claim that this is not always a change for the better. On the largest scale, historians point to a shift from work on the land to days spent in factories. As the technological revolution continued, there came to be fewer jobs in industry and more in services such as finance, catering or healthcare. Large areas of countryside have given way to massive urban sprawls, and this has environmental impacts. More people live in cities than ever before. This might offer more facilities, but does it also reduce quality of life?

The Cray supercomputer is one of the most advanced in the world. It was developed to help process information gained at CERN, the European centre for particle physics in Switzerland.

Supercomputers

The advantages and disadvantages of technology at work vary from case to case, and the ethical questions are far from easily answered. Machines can take over repetitive or dangerous jobs. Sometimes the work left for people to do will be more skilled, sometimes less. Sometimes they will earn more, sometimes less. It all depends on exactly what the machines are designed to do. One of the biggest fears is that eventually a robot will be created that can do everything a human can – and more. Extremely intelligent computers, supercomputers, already exist and are being constantly improved. What will the future hold for humans if we create something that effectively renders us obsolete?

> ❝ *Supercomputers will achieve one human brain capacity by 2010, and personal computers will do so by about 2020.* ❞
>
> *Ray Kurzweil*
> *American scientist*

Artificial intelligence

As computers become faster and programmes more efficient, many forecasters predict that machines could be built with intelligence to rival humans in our lifetime. This would be a new stage of technology – artificial intelligence. Although this is something only seen in films at the moment, it is not impossible that one day soon devices of our own making may end up having rights and duties now only regarded as relevant to people. Is it ethically right for scientists to be developing super-intelligent robots? If they are indeed super-intelligent, how can we ensure they look after human Interests? These are important questions to address before technology advances beyond the point of no return.

Social robots

Quite advanced 'social' robots – those that interact and communicate with humans – have already been created. American robot-maker Cynthia Breazeal has designed Leonardo, a furry, gremlinoid creature. Leonardo has 32 motors to move different parts of its face, and will one day be able to see, hear, speak and feel. At the moment work is mainly focusing on giving it facial expressions that react to what people say or do. Breazeal has conducted experiments that show that that people feel more attached to Leonardo than to a computer animation that just looks like Leonardo. They seem to see a real creature. Other social robots include eMuu and iCat, both developed at the Eindhoven University of Technology in the Netherlands. There seems little harm in these interactive robots, but while they are a novelty at the moment, should we be more aware of the risks their technology may lead to in the future?

> **Replacing human contact with a machine is an awful idea. But some people have no contact at all. If the choice is going to be a nursing home or staying at home with a robot, we think people will choose the robot.**

Sebastian Thrum
Assistant professor of computer science, Carnegie Mellon University, USA

Leonardo can understand some language and can learn simple tasks from humans, such as pressing buttons.

Specialised robots

Before social robots become commonplace, it is more likely that we will see greater use of robots for complex, specialised tasks.

One of the best recent examples of how specialised robots can be used is their use in pharmacies, where drug dispensing is now often automated. Robot drug dispensers read a prescription from a barcode, select one of hundreds of drugs in their store, and count out the right number of pills into a vial that is labelled for the patient. The process takes less time than a human pharmacist, and makes it easier to keep track of drug stocks and use-by dates.

Robots like this could reduce the need for pharmacists, but there is still plenty of work left for them in hospitals, where they get to spend more time with patients who have more complicated prescriptions. The machines are now widely used in big hospital pharmacies and are starting to appear in some high-street chemists as well.

Robots are now being used in pharmacies. They can find prescriptions among the packets on shelves from data that has been input remotely, from a hospital or doctor's surgery.

THE ROBOT ETHICS CHARTER

South Korea is one of the leading nations in the development of robotics technology, and it has been predicted that by 2020 every household in Korea will have a robot to perform domestic tasks. In 2007, the South Korean government announced it was supporting the creation of a Robot Ethics Charter. This will outline how robots will be made and what their roles and functions will be. The charter is intended to safeguard against the potential dangers of intelligent machines, but also to prevent humans abusing robots.

Understanding the issues

There are many ways of finding out about new technological developments and the associated ethical issues. You can read about them every day in the newspapers or you can research them on the Internet. From there it is possible to make informed choices about what technology you will support (perhaps by going out and buying it), and which you disagree with. But can we all have a say in what kinds of new technologies are developed, or what risks we are prepared to live with? It is not easy to get into conversation with the experts, but there are several ways in which the public can get involved.

> 66 *Global technologies can, particularly in the long term, be of greater significance than prime ministers or presidents.* 99
>
> **Dr Doug Parr**
> *Greenpeace UK*

Gathering information

An opinion survey gathers information from many people (usually around 1,000). The questions are usually fairly simple, and results can depend on how they are asked. 'Would you rather have new nuclear power stations or freeze in the dark?', for example, will get a different response to 'Would you prefer nuclear, coal or renewable energy?' In this way, public responses can be manipulated to meet the requirements of the organisation conducting the survey.

An alternative is to organise longer discussions with a smaller number of people. This does not tell you what a statistical sample of the whole population thinks, like an opinion poll, but it can show what kinds of factors people want taken into account – what they really care about. Sometimes, these discussions can become elaborate, as in the so-called 'consensus conference', where a group of people comes together several times. This has been pioneered in Denmark by the Danish Board of Technology. In such discussions the subject is studied and technical experts are on hand to

s Fogh Rasmussen
ter of Denmark

Bjørn Lomborg
Director, The Environmental Assessment Institute

This consensus conference in Denmark was held to discuss environmental issues. Such conferences are now a popular forum for addressing ethical questions in science and technology.

answer questions, and then all work together on a final report. These meetings have since been used to discuss many technological issues in a number of countries.

Whatever method is adopted, there is still the issue of how all the information gathered is used. Should it be taken up lock, stock and barrel? Or should it be considered as one input among many? People may expect their views to be acted on and become disillusioned if they are not. Deciding how to decide is one of the biggest questions that developments in technology has given rise to.

Organisations like the UK Youth Parliament allow young people to express their opinions about many different issues, particularly how they would like ethical questions to be addressed.

UK YOUTH PARLIAMENT

In March 2006, 70 young people aged 13 to 18 met in the UK Youth Parliament in Birmingham, England to hear and talk about nanotechnologies. The day-long event included an electronic quiz, votes before and after the discussion, workshops with specialists and discussion with a member of parliament. The day was one of a series of events aimed at finding out what people think about nanotechnology while most applications are still at an early stage.

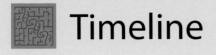

Timeline

1811
The Luddite movement is formed in England in opposition to new technologies, such as factory machines, which are believed to be putting people out of work.

1921
The first robot is built, marking the beginning of artificial life forms.

1930
The 'differential analyser' – an early analogue computer – is built by Vannevar Bush.

1941
The Z3 becomes the first computer to be controlled by software.

1945
The atomic bomb is created and then dropped on the cities of Hiroshima and Nagasaki in Japan. The widespread devastation effectively ends the Second World War.

1961
The first industrial robot is used in a car-production factory in New Jersey, United States.

1972
The United States and the Soviet Union sign an anti-ballistic missile treaty, limiting the development of remote weapons.

1973
The Ethernet, a local computer network, is created.

1985
British scientist Alec Jeffreys works out the basic principles of DNA fingerprinting, which later becomes a key component of forensic science.

1989
The World Wide Web is launched, connecting computers all over the world.

1999
The free music file-sharing site Napster is launched.

2002
The Massachusetts Institute of Technology is awarded $50 million to develop a new type of body armour that will protect soldiers against the effects of chemical and biological warfare.

2005
The US Supreme Court rules that music file-sharing websites can be sued by record companies if users share files that are under copyright. Google establishes a China-based service as part of its search engine, to cooperate with the Chinese government in limiting access to certain information.

2006
The Bill and Melinda Gates Foundation pledges $328 million to provide access to computers and the Internet for developing countries.

2007
Forty-six nations sign a declaration agreeing to a ban on the production, trade and stockpiling of cluster bombs by 2008.

Further Information

● Books

Digital Technology by Chris Woodford, Evans Brothers Ltd, 2006

Modern Bombs by Steve D. White, Children's Press, 2006

Nanotechnology by Dianne Maddox, Blackbirch Press, 2005

Nanotechnology by Rebecca L. Johnson, Lerner Publications, 2005

New Technology series by various authors, Evans Brothers, 2008

● Websites

www.army-technology.com/projects/
Defence industry website that provides information on weapons systems under development.

www.ifr.org/index.asp
International Federation of Robotics website, which has statistics and news about industrial robots.

www.aspcr.com/
American Society for Prevention of Cruelty to Robots.

www.wired.com/wired/archive/8.04/joy_pr.html
Computer scientist Bill Joy's essay 'Why the Future Doesn't Need Us'.

Glossary

artificial intelligence computer science that focuses on ways of giving machines levels of intelligence similar to that of humans.

automation the process of creating machines that can move and work by themselves, so they are fully automatic.

ballistic missile a weapon-delivery mechanism; ballistic missiles are remote weapons that are programmed to a particular course, which cannot be altered after launch.

biological warfare the use of organisms that produce disease in humans or animals as a weapon; biological weapons are often bacteria, viruses or toxins (poisons).

biometrics science and technology that relates to biological data – those that measure human characteristics such as fingerprints, iris patterns or voice patterns.

chemical warfare military operations that use chemicals to kill or injure people.

closed-circuit television (CCTV) a surveillance system in which cameras are connected to television monitors; they are viewed in a closed area such as a shop rather than being publicly distributed.

Cold War the name given to the period of political and military tension between the United States and the Soviet Union from the end of the Second World War until the 1990s.

copyright the law that grants exclusive rights to someone for a piece of music, writing or art; it means that no one else can copy it without permission of the copyright holder.

cyberspace a word coined by William Gibson in his book *Neuromancer*. Today it is usually used to refer to information networks available through computers, such as the Internet.

database a collection of related knowledge, often held on computer, that allows the user easy access to certain information.

defoliant a chemical that destroys leaves and plants. Used by the military to destroy tree cover and reveal where the enemy might be hiding.

DNA (deoxyribonucleic acid) the chemical material that makes up genes. DNA is a large molecule that carries the genetic code to make proteins, which determine characteristics.

enzyme a protein that speeds up chemical reactions in living organisms.

ethics a formalised set of rules generally developed from widely held morals. Ethical codes may become accepted by a whole society, when they often develop into laws (see *morals*).

fossil fuels resources such as coal and oil that were formed in the past from the remains of animals and plants (fossils). Humans are currently using up fossil fuels faster than the Earth can replenish them.

hacker someone who 'hacks' into computer systems remotely to gain access to information they are not authorised to see.

laser light amplification by stimulated emission of radiation. Lasers are powerful beams of light that produce intense heat.

Luddite term used to refer to someone who is against the development of new technologies. The name comes from a nineteenth-century group who destroyed factory machinery because they felt it was putting people out of work.

mass production the large-scale creation of a particular product, usually through means of a production or assembly line, in which the end products are identical to one another.

morals a set of beliefs held by an individual. Morals may come from religious beliefs or the values of the individual (see *ethics*).

munitions materials of war, such as weapons and ammunition.

nanometre one billionth – one thousand millionth – of a metre.

nanotechnology technology that deals with the creation of tiny mechanical devices at a molecular level.

napalm a type of 'jelly' made from acids mixed with petroleum, which sets fire to anything it touches. It is often used as a weapon.

NATO (North Atlantic Treaty Organisation) an organisation formed in 1949 as a defence against the spread of Communism after the Second World War and the potential threat of military attack. There are now 189 NATO countries.

pesticide a chemical sprayed on crops to kill pests that might destroy them.

pirate to copy something, such as music or a film, without getting permission to do so.

plagiarism copying other people's work or claiming their ideas and pretending they are your own.

renewable resources resources such as the sun, wind and water, that are continually replenished and will not run out.

robot a mechanical device that can perform some of the tasks that humans can, and which is not directly under human control.

satellite a man-made device that orbits the Earth, often used in communications.

UNESCO the United Nations Educational, Scientific and Cultural Organisation – a body that promotes education and communication in the arts and sciences among countries that are members of the United Nations.

virus a computer program designed to spread quickly, usually via email, and that causes systems to crash and data to be lost.

Index